SCHIRMER'S LIBRARY
OF MUSICAL CLASSICS

WOLFGANG AMADEUS MOZART

Trios

For Piano, Violin and Violoncello

[No. VII for Piano, Violin (or Clarinet) and Viola]

Trio I, in G major [K. 496]
Library Volume 1602

Trio II, in B♭ major [K. 502]
Library Volume 1603

Trio III, in E major [K. 542]
Library Volume 1604

Trio IV, in C major [K. 548]
Library Volume 1605

Trio V, in G major [K. 564]
Library Volume 1606

Trio VI, in B♭ major [K. 254]
Library Volume 1607

Trio VII, in E♭ major [K. 498]
Library Volume 1403

Trio VIII, in D minor [K. 442]
Library Volume 1608

ISBN 0-7935-5237-0

G. SCHIRMER, Inc.

DISTRIBUTED BY

HAL•LEONARD®
CORPORATION
7777 W. BLUEMOUND RD. P.O. BOX 13819 MILWAUKEE, WI 53213

T0051131

Trio VII
In E♭ Major
[Köchel, No. 498]

W. A. Mozart
Edited by Joseph Adamowski

4

29627

29627

Trio

29627

29627

Trio VII
In Eb Major
[Köchel, No. 498]

Viola

W. A. Mozart
Edited by Joseph Adamowski

29627 d

Viola

Viola

Viola

Viola

Viola

Viola

VIOLIN

ISBN 0-7935-5237-0

G. SCHIRMER, Inc.

DISTRIBUTED BY

HAL•LEONARD®
CORPORATION

7777 W. BLUEMOUND RD. P.O. BOX 13819 MILWAUKEE, WI 53213

Trio VII
In E♭ Major
[Köchel, No. 498]

Violin

W. A. Mozart
Edited by Joseph Adamowski

Violin

29627 a

Violin

Violin

Allegretto (♩ = 120)

29627 a

next page

Violin

Violin

CLARINET I

ISBN 0-7935-5237-0

G. SCHIRMER, Inc.

DISTRIBUTED BY

HAL•LEONARD®
CORPORATION
7777 W. BLUEMOUND RD. P.O. BOX 13819 MILWAUKEE, WI 53213

Trio VII
In E♭ Major
[Köchel, No. 498]

Clarinet in B♭

Edited by Carl Deis

W. A. Mozart
Edited by Joseph Adamowski

Clarinet in B♭

Clarinet in B♭

Clarinet in B♭

next page

Clarinet in B♭

Clarinet in B♭

29627b